THE
BIG-ASS
SWEAR WORD
COLORING BOOK

FRESH
OUT
OF
FUCKS

Why the
hell not?

The fucking sun will come out tomorrow

LET
THAT
SHIT
GO

BE
AWESOME
★ AND ★
GIVE NO
FUCKS

Fuck it, let's color!

CARPE
FUCKING
DIEM

THE BIG-ASS SWEAR WORD COLORING BOOK

A F*CKING Ton of Uplifting SH*T to Color and Display

ST. MARTIN'S GRIFFIN
NEW YORK

THE BIG-ASS SWEAR WORD COLORING BOOK.

Copyright © 2018 by St. Martin's Press. All rights reserved.
Printed in the United States of America. For information, address
St. Martin's Press, 175 Fifth Avenue, New York, N.Y. 10010.

THE BIG-ASS SWEAR WORD COLORING BOOK is a compilation of materials published in
the volumes CHEER THE F*CK UP, MOMMY DRINKS BECAUSE YOU CRY, and F*CK, YEAH!

www.stmartins.com

ISBN: 978-1-250-18314-9 (trade paperback)

Our books may be purchased in bulk for promotional, educational,
or business use. Please contact your local bookseller or the
Macmillan Corporate and Premium Sales Department at
1-800-221-7945, extension 5442, or by e-mail
at MacmillanSpecialMarkets@macmillan.com.

First Edition: July 2018

10 9 8

KEEP CALM AND
CARRY THE FUCK ON

Suck it up,
buttercup

SHIT HAPPENS

Tomorrow's a
new day
to be your best
damn self

Quit slackin' and make shit happen

WHY THE HELL NOT?

Live the shit out of life

IT'S A
FAN-FUCKING-TASTIC
DAY

Smile, asshole!

BE YOUR OWN MOTHERFUCKING HERO

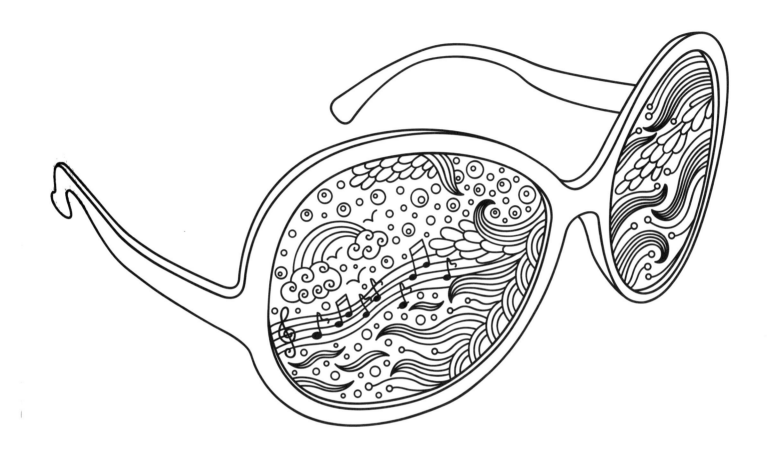

YOU ARE A RAY OF
FUCKING SUNSHINE

When life hands you lemons,
squeeze those bitches into your vodka

YOU MAY FEEL LIKE SHIT,
BUT YOU LOOK
FUCKING FANTASTIC

PRINCESS
FUCK·IT·ALL

Life is about kicking ass,
not kissing it

The fucking sun will
come out tomorrow

YOU'RE BEAUTIFUL, BITCHES!

CARPE
FUCKING
DIEM

Resting bitch face keeps you pretty

NOBODY DOES IT
FUCKING BETTER
THAN YOU

KEEP THAT SHIT UP!

When I get
out of bed in
the morning,
the devil says,
"Oh shit, she's up."

Be awesome
and give no fucks

GO THROUGH SHIT, GROW THROUGH SHIT

Holy shitballs, you're awesome

Make every
fucking day count

FUCK IT, LET'S COLOR!

DO EPIC SHIT

FUCK WHAT THEY THINK

Enjoy this lovely fucking day

Blow your own damn mind

RISE, SHINE, AND KICK ASS

RISE, SHINE, AND KICK ASS

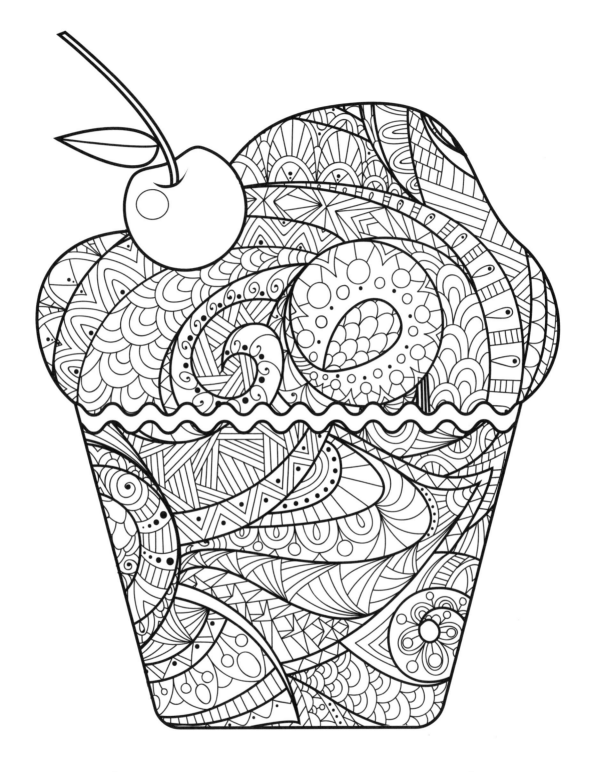

You're someone's
reason to masturbate

Let out your inner bitch

If I throw a stick, will you leave?

NEVER FUCK
WITH THE QUEEN

Less bitter,
more glitter

I'm feeling a bit overworked and under-intoxicated.

SORRY I RUINED YOUR LIFE BY ASKING YOU TO PUT YOUR SHOES AWAY

"Trust me, you can dance."

—Vodka

Remember when I asked
for your opinion?
Yeah, me neither.

Fantastic as fuck

BE NICE TO YOUR CHILDREN, FOR THEY WILL CHOOSE YOUR RETIREMENT HOME.

BRAVE
BADASS

How about never?
Is never good for you?

It's a
beautiful
fucking
day

I child-proofed the house, but they still get in.

I hate housework!
You make the beds, do the dishes,
and six months later
you have to do it all over again!

GRAB LIFE BY THE BALLS

I hear you. I'm just not listening.

Your wedding plans sound really interesting to you.

8 hours of labor means

I'm always right

MY IDEA OF A HAPPY MEAL IS A BOTTLE OF VODKA, 2 XANAX AND A COOKIE

Today's Mood: Bitch with a chance of sarcasm

YOU ARE ABOUT TO EXCEED
THE LIMITS OF MY MEDICATION

You don't get
the ass you want
by sitting on it

I'm eating
my feelings
and they're
absolutely
delicious.

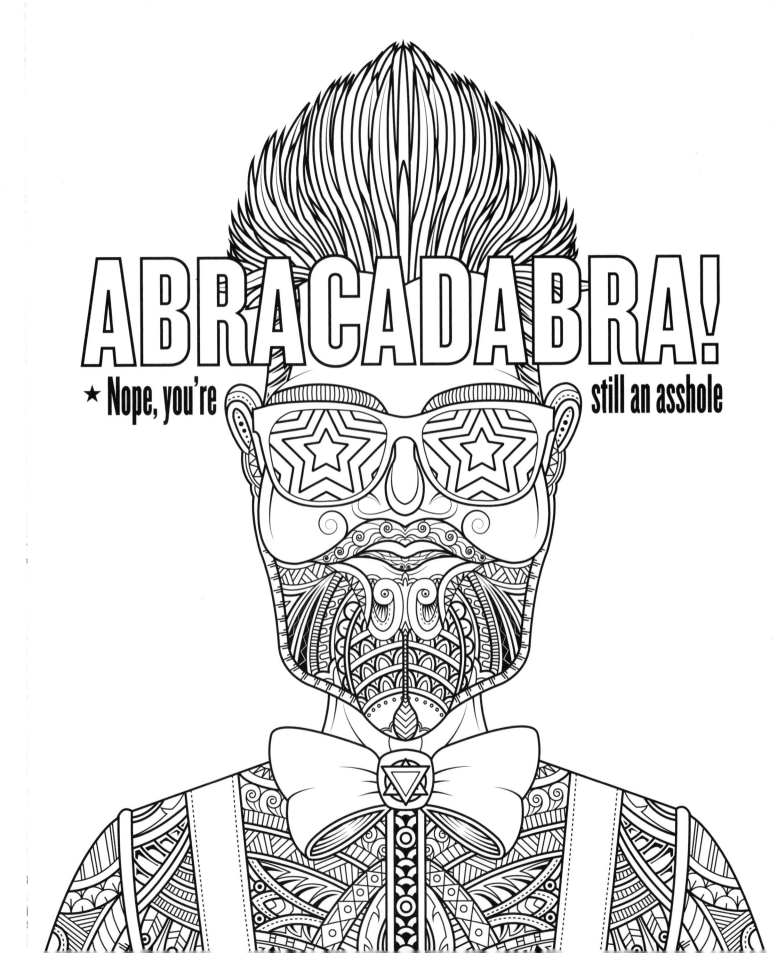

I love cleaning up messes I didn't make, so I became a mom.

YOU PROBABLY NEED THESE, TOO

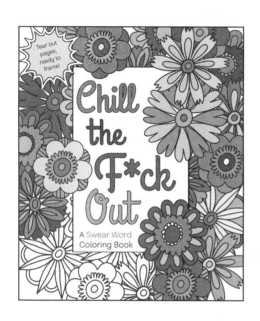

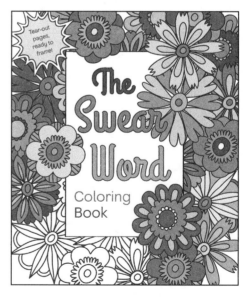